Good-

Written by Rozanne Lanczak Williams
Created by Sue Lewis
Illustrated by Patty Briles

Creative Teaching Press

Good-bye!
© 2002 Creative Teaching Press, Inc.
Written by Rozanne Lanczak Williams
Illustrated by Patty Briles
Project Manager: Sue Lewis
Project Director: Carolea Williams

Published in the United States of America by:
Creative Teaching Press, Inc.
P.O. Box 2723
Huntington Beach, CA 92647-0723

All rights reserved. No part of this book may be reproduced in any form without the written permission of Creative Teaching Press, Inc.

CTP 3220

Good-bye, goldfish!

Good-bye, goose!

Good-bye, gorilla!

Good-bye, garage!

Good-bye, garden!

Good-bye, gate!

Guess where I am going.

I am going
to Grandma's house!

Create your own book!

Make a suitcase-shaped book cover and pages. Write and illustrate your own good-bye book. Use *g* words and other words you know.

Words in *Good-bye!*

Initial Consonant: *g*	High-Frequency Words	Other
good-bye	I	where
goldfish	am	house
goose	to	
gorilla		
garage		
garden		
gate		
guess		
Grandma's		
going		